The Secret World of BIRD NESTS

Lucy Menzies
Illustrated by Namasri Niumim

t&h

CONTENTS

A WORLD OF NESTS 4
Why do birds build nests?

CUP NEST 6
Simple and effective

DOMED NEST 8
Prickly protection

WOVEN NEST 10
Nest to impress

MOUND NEST 12
Build your own island

STITCHED NEST 14
Perfectly tailored

SCRAPE NEST 16
Scratch and splatter

TUNNEL NEST 18
For birds that burrow

SEALED NEST 20
Peekaboo!

FLOATING NEST 22
Safe in the swamp

PLATFORM NEST 24
A room with a view

INDOOR NEST 26
Brooding in a barn

SOCIABLE NEST 28
Community living

HERMIT NEST 30
A hidden hangout

EDIBLE NEST 32
Would you eat a nest made of spit?

MUD NEST 34
A mud pie castle

INCUBATOR NEST 36
Toasty eggs

CLAY NEST 38
Eggs in an oven

PENDULUM NEST 40
Making an entrance

BOWER POWER 42
A decorative display

NEST BUILDERS 44
How to build a cup nest

GLOSSARY 46

INDEX 47

A WORLD OF NESTS

WHY DO BIRDS BUILD NESTS?

You may have spotted a nest hidden away in the boughs of a tree in your neighbourhood. Or maybe when you think of a nest, you picture a clutch of eggs in a cosy chicken coop, attended to by a mother hen. But across the world, billions of birds are building all kinds of different nests.

Like all animals, birds need safe places to shelter within their natural habitats. Different birds have adapted their nest building to suit the type of environment they live in and make use of materials that are found there. That's why there is so much variety in the structures they build. Whether they need to keep cool in hot weather or defend themselves from deadly predators, birds have developed problem-solving methods to build nests so their chicks will survive and thrive.

In this book, you'll discover 18 kinds of nests from all over the globe and meet the birds that build them. You might even be shocked by some of their techniques – from borrowing the silk of spider webs to creating homes made with their own spit!

Next time you see a nest out in the wild, you'll know all about the skill, instinct and hard work that went into its creation.

WHAT ARE NESTS FOR?

Most birds build nests as a safe place to lay eggs and raise their hatchlings until they are old enough to leave the nest. A few birds live in their nests all year round, but many will find other shelter – such as a hollow tree – to sleep in until the breeding season rolls around once more.

ADMIRE FROM AFAR

If you see a nest in the wild, it's important not to touch it – or even get too close. Sometimes a bird will abandon its nest if it feels scared – even with its eggs inside. To avoid spooking birds, be sure to keep your distance.

CUP NEST

SIMPLE AND EFFECTIVE

A female Song Thrush carefully watches over her 5 beautiful greenish-blue eggs – a shocking colour amongst the surrounding greenery, but luckily they're out of sight enough to be safe. To cradle her eggs, the thrush has sculpted a cup-shaped nest, the most common type of bird nest found in nature.

To make it, she first wedged twigs into the fork of a laurel tree. The tangled twigs were knotted together to create a solid platform to build her nest on. Once the platform was ready, she threaded together dried grasses, twisting them upwards with her beak to form a cup. The bird then camouflaged the outside of the nest with green moss and leaves to keep it hidden amongst the trees to protect her eggs from hungry predators.

Next, she strengthened the structure with layers of rotten wood and mud to create a dry, hard inner lining. Other birds would have then added fine grasses to cushion their cup nests, but not the Song Thrush – it may not sound as comfy, but the hard mud lining keeps her nest just as warm as those made by other thrushes and requires less effort and time to build. Finally, the bird pressed her body down, over and over, into the inner lining of the nest, smoothing and settling it. And with that, the nesting season had begun!

DOMED NEST

PRICKLY PROTECTION

A shock of plant fibres sits in the nook of a prickly pear cactus. It might look like a tangled mess – and it is! – but it's also the carefully-crafted nest of the Cactus Wren. This bird makes its home in the hot, dusty deserts of the US and Mexico. The year-round heat here means that the wren doesn't have to migrate. While other birds fly to warmer climates in winter months, the Cactus Wren stays put.

But it's not all sunshine – danger lurks close by as snakes search for tasty eggs to eat. As a defence from these hunters, Cactus Wrens build their nests in the spiky arms of cacti, such as jumping chollas – or in this case, a prickly pear. The wren cleverly chooses a spot angled towards cooling winds, which bring relief from the beating sun. Among the spines of the cactus, she uses twigs, roots and dry grasses to construct a large, domed nest about the size and shape of a rugby ball. Its rounded form means that her young will be completely concealed at all times, protected from predators and the elements. The inner nest is tube-shaped, making it hard for larger animals to get past the entrance. Next, the wren carefully lines the thick inner walls with soft feathers and grasses. This will keep her chicks warm during the cold, harsh nights.

Now, it's time for the Cactus Wren to lay her eggs. But she won't rest for long afterwards. She has more eggs to lay this year, so more nests need to be built. Her mate is already constructing one, and soon she will be back at work to help him.

WOVEN NEST

NEST TO IMPRESS

A striking bird flits from branch to branch in the South African shrubland. Outside of the breeding season, his plumage is a dull olive-yellow colour, but now he is dressed to impress – with a distinctive black bill and face, and brilliantly yellow head and underparts. He's a Southern Masked-Weaver, and he's looking for somewhere to build nests to attract a potential mate's attention.

As the name suggests, this bird weaves nests. He chooses an acacia tree branch close to a lake on which to build. He then places pieces of grass onto the branch to form a base ring. With more grass and reeds, he continues to expertly knit an orb-shaped nest that will hang droopily, like a pendulum in a clock.

His potential mate, the female weaver, has been watching him the whole time. Once he's mostly finished, it's down to her to judge his handiwork. She has very high standards, so he may have to build several more nests before she's impressed enough to climb inside – a sign that she accepts the nest, and the male as her mate. The female will then cushion the inside with soft grasses, feathers and leaves, creating a cosy and safe space to lay her eggs. But the work isn't over yet. These birds live in colonies, and male Southern Masked-Weavers often have more than one mate, meaning he'll have many more nests to build!

MOUND NEST

BUILD YOUR OWN ISLAND

The sun reflects off the still waters of Laguna Miñiques, a lake high up in the Andes mountain range in Chile. The terrain here feels almost like another planet – it's sparse and rocky, with little vegetation around. About 4 metres from the shore sits a small island, just peeping out of the water. It's jagged, craggy and slick with slimy green algae. But it's not an island – it's a nest! A mated pair of Horned Coots have built it together.

They have made hundreds of trips to collect rocks and pile them up in the lake, facing stiff competition from other coots also on the same mission for materials. It's an enormous undertaking, as the stones used to make the nest can weigh as much as 1.5 tonnes in total. Though only its peak is visible above the surface, the huge, cone-shaped nest spreads out beneath the water, similar in shape to the nearby volcanoes that tower over the lake.

The female Horned Coot lays 3 to 5 eggs at the top of the nest in a crater that has been padded with aquatic plants. Because the water here is so calm, the eggs are in no danger from waves, and the nest can be used again and again over many breeding seasons. Though this mound nest isn't a perfect design – the eggs are in plain sight above the water, so they're a target for hunters, both animal and human alike.

1. The female bird chooses her leaves.

2. She stitches the leaves together.

STITCHED NEST

PERFECTLY TAILORED

A pair of Common Tailorbirds dart around a forest in Sri Lanka, the green and brown of their feathers blending in with the lush surroundings. Their name is appropriate – today, the female will start sewing her nest. It's a fiddly job that usually takes 4 days.

The materials for this stitched nest have been gathered by the male bird, but the female does the crafting. She creates the base of the nest from leaves that are still attached to a lush mango tree. The leaves must be the right size, so the bird wraps them around her body to check the measurements.

Satisfied with the fit, she then folds the leaves and pierces tiny holes along the outer edges with her slim, needle-like beak. In her beak she holds a fine thread made from natural materials, such as fibres from a cotton plant or the silk from a spider's web. She carefully weaves the thread in and out of the holes, sewing the sides of the leaves together to make a snug little pocket. This is delicate work – if a leaf tears, the bird will work tirelessly on repairs, or she may need to start all over again.

Once the pocket has been stitched, the female stuffs it with soft plant fibres, feathers and fur, to build a secret inner nest where she will lay her eggs.

3. She adds a soft lining to the nest.

CLEVER CAMOUFLAGE

The nest is so well camouflaged amongst the tree's foliage that it's very hard to spot. Instead, listen closely for the chirrups of the hatchlings!

SCRAPE NEST

SCRATCH AND SPLATTER

Along the shores of the Galápagos Islands in the Pacific Ocean, a Blue-footed Booby wanders toward a small hollow that has been scraped into the ground. It barely looks like a nest at all – made of only the rocky soil, with no camouflage to cover it. It's encircled with a ring of white splatters. This is guano, or bird poo, that has been sprayed around to mark a booby's territory.

Two eggs have been laid here. The male and female birds take turns keeping the eggs warm, using their turquoise feet as heat pads. Boobies don't have many predators on the island, so the eggs should be relatively safe. But once the chicks hatch, they'll have each other to worry about! They're a feisty bunch, fighting – and sometimes killing – each other as they compete to be fed the most food by their parents.

BEST FOOT FORWARD

Bright blue feet are a sign that a male booby is young, fit and good at raising chicks, so females choose a mate with the most eye-popping flippers. During courtship, the male attempts to entice the female with a dance called 'displaying'. He'll raise his wings and tilt his beak to the sky, all while flashing his fancy footwear.

TUNNEL NEST

FOR BIRDS THAT BURROW

Along the bank of a slow-moving stream in Wales, all is quiet except for the soft burble of the water as it gently trickles along, gleaming in the spring sunshine. It's a peaceful spot to relax...unless you're a kingfisher!

A pair of Common Kingfishers have spent all day flying in and out of their burrow, hidden in the sandy bank above the stream, to deliver fish to their hungry brood. Each chick can eat up to 18 fish a day. So, the parents must catch over 70 fish today to feed them all.

These birds are no strangers to hard work. Before their chicks came along, they both spent 12 long days building their burrow, which measures around 60 cm in length – a huge task for little birds like these.

The kingfishers slowly carved out the tunnel by pecking at the soft soil with their long beaks, over and over and over again, using their feet to shovel back excess soil.

At the end of the tunnel is a small, rounded chamber where the female kingfisher lays her eggs, safely out of the reach of predators. Once hatched, the chicks will stay in the burrow for around 25 days, until they are big enough to start fishing for themselves.

Neither the tunnel nor the chamber is padded with lining during construction, but over time, a lining forms naturally. As the chicks are fed with fish, the nest becomes strewn with leftover bones, rotting fish and bird poo. It's rather a smelly place to grow up in – but there's no place like home!

The tunnel is sloped so that waste can flow out of the chamber, like a sewer. A greenish, sludgy liquid of bird poo and rotting fish slips towards the entrance.

SEALED NEST

PEEKABOO!

From the hollow of a tree trunk, a single eye peeps out through a small hole. It belongs to a female Great Hornbill, encased in her nest and eagerly awaiting the return of her mate, carrying her dinner.

The pair of hornbills picked the cavity in this tree as a secure spot for a nest. At the time, the opening was large enough for the female to climb through. Once snugly inside, she sealed herself in, filling the entrance with her own droppings until only a small slot remained – just big enough for a beak to pass through. This is a defence against predators here in the Himalayas, such as the Yellow-Throated Marten. Any invaders that can fit through the nest's slot should be small enough for the bird to scare away – or even kill – herself.

Safe in her nest, the bird sheds her flight feathers because she doesn't need them in her woodland fortress. She will lay her eggs and stay here until it's time for her babies to leave the nest. Until then, it's up to the male hornbill to feed her and the chicks, taking endless trips back and forth for food.

As well as being an opening for meals to be passed into, the slot is used as a toilet by the inhabitants, as they squirt their droppings out of it. This hole is also important for controlling airflow in and out of the hollow, keeping it a safe temperature for the birds. Once it's time to leave – after 4 long months of enclosure – the female hornbill will use her mighty beak to crack the opening and smash her way to freedom. Her chicks will stay in the nest for a few more days until they're ready to fly.

FLOATING NEST

SAFE IN THE SWAMP

In the Northern Territory of Australia, a Magpie Goose is hard at work making a nest. The male goose does most of the crafting, but the female will occasionally chip in to help. Magpie Geese are wetland birds found in swamps and floodplains.

They live together in large flocks – or colonies. To build their nests on the water, Magpie Geese create intricate floating platforms out of reeds and grasses that grow in the swamp. The roots of these plants stop the nests from floating away.

1. The Magpie Goose uses its beak and long neck to grasp reeds by their stems and bend them down into the water.

2. The bird moves round in a circle, bending reeds, trampling them down with its feet and using its beak to weave them into a circular, floating platform.

3. The goose keeps working in this way, folding and trampling to make the platform thick and sturdy.

4. Finally, reeds are piled up into a thatched mound, with a deep, unlined cup-shaped dip in the middle to hold the eggs.

WATER BABIES

Just 24 hours after hatching, the goslings are usually ready to leave the nest and head into the water. Even though they are natural swimmers, goslings still need their parents to protect and feed them, and they will live together as a family until the next breeding season.

PLATFORM NEST

A ROOM WITH A VIEW

Perched right at the top of a tall tree is a majestic Bald Eagle, the king of the skies. She is sitting in her nest, called an eyrie. As a bird of prey, the eagle needs to have an excellent view of its hunting ground, and this mammoth nest provides a full panoramic scope of the snow-covered forest here in Alaska, USA. The nest is near a lake, as it's around water that the eagle hunts for fish, waterfowl and other small animals.

Supported by the thick trunk of a Sitka spruce, the nest is made up of sticks that the eagle and her mate drop into place. They fix and fiddle with the twigs, rearranging them until things are just right. This creates an enormous platform for the birds to survey their surroundings from. The nest is extremely heavy – the largest recorded Bald Eagle nest was 2.9 m wide, 6 m deep, and weighed more than 2 tonnes! It is lined with soft moss, grass, plants and sometimes even seaweed, to create protective padding for eggs.

The nest is so huge that there's plenty of room for the eagles and their eggs, so even though it is very high up, there's little danger of the hatchlings falling out. These birds will reuse the nest for up to 35 years. With a view as magnificent as this, it's no wonder they keep coming back.

INDOOR NEST

BROODING IN A BARN

Here in the north of England, it's nighttime on the farm, and the moon is shining brightly. In this cosy barn, the animals are softly sleeping. The pigs are cuddling up together in the hay, the donkeys have bedded down for a good rest and the cows are snoozing while standing up.

But there are other hidden residents in the building. Tucked high in the rafters is a brood of Barn Swallows in a mud nest. To make their nests, male and female swallows gather mud in their mouths and combine it with grass and their own saliva to make brick-like pellets to build with. First, they paste the mud pellets to a beam to create a ledge on which to stand. From there, they mould a bumpy, pocket-shaped nest, about half the size of a grapefruit. The nest is then lined with soft feathers. It takes up to 3 weeks to build a nest, so swallows compete to reuse old nests as much as they can.

The mother swallow swiftly darts in and out of the barn – catching insects in mid-air to feed her young. The chicks cheep noisily, their mouths gawping expectantly as they peep their heads out of the nest.

WORLD TRAVELLERS

Barn Swallows can be found all over the world, on all continents. These swallows will migrate all the way from England to Africa to find food and avoid harsh weather.

MOVING IN

Swallows used to build their nests in caves or on the edge of cliffs, but that's rare these days. When humans started building shelters like barns, the swallows decided to move in too.

SOCIABLE NEST

COMMUNITY LIVING

A lush, green camel thorn tree stands out from the dry and dusty landscape here in South Africa. Hanging from its boughs is an enormous structure: a bumpy, lumpy nest that weighs up to 1 tonne and can be around 4 m deep and over 7 m in length.

This nest has been made by a colony of Sociable Weavers. These little birds make some of the largest nests in the world, capable of housing up to 400 Sociable Weavers. Like a block of flats, each family of birds lives in their own separate nesting chamber within the nest.

To start building the nest, an extended family of birds – 2 to 3 pairs – use twigs to construct a secure roof, anchored around horizontal tree branches. From there, each pair of birds in the colony builds their own chamber from dry grasses, cushioning it with downy feathers and fur. As the colony grows over generations, new chambers are added to the bottom of the nest, and the birds work together to make the roof larger. Sometimes a nest can get so big that the tree buckles under the weight of it.

BIRD B&B

Sociable Weaver nests also provide homes for other birds, including the South African Pygmy Falcon. Larger birds such as vultures sometimes nest of the roof too. The weavers don't mind as these birds are added predator protection – and there's plenty of room!

The underside of the nest is pronged with sharp sticks to defend the birds from predators such as tree snakes. The thick thatch also helps keep the birds cool in the heat and warm on cold nights. Thanks to the birds' constant repairs and upkeep, these nests can survive for a hundred years.

LOOK UP!

If you stand below the nest and look up, you'll see just how intricate it really is. Each interwoven chamber has its own entrance.

HERMIT NEST

A HIDDEN HANGOUT

Deep within the thick, shaded understory of the Costa Rican rainforest, a Green Hermit hummingbird hovers around the entrance to her nest, wings beating up to 80 times per second. Her iridescent feathers shimmer in the sunlight. The nest, known as a hermit nest, has been attached to the drooping leaf of a palm tree that hangs over a stream. The leaf bobs as the bird climbs aboard, returning to her clutch of eggs.

The cone-shaped nest is made of plant fibres, which the female has stuck onto the leaf using spider webs as a sticky glue. She worked alone to make it, but now shares it with two jelly bean-shaped eggs. It's a snug fit in the nest. Being on the underside of the leaf means the nest is hidden from view and well camouflaged. The bending leaf also acts as a roof, sheltering the bird from downpours during Costa Rica's rainy season.

EDIBLE NEST

WOULD YOU EAT A NEST MADE OF SPIT?

In Sarawak, Malaysia, a wall of the deep, dark Niah Caves is lined with thousands of little, white pockets. These are the nests of a colony of White-nest Swiftlets, huddled together for security. The nests are truly amazing structures, each made entirely from the birds' own saliva!

When it's time to breed, the White-nest Swiftlets' saliva glands become bigger, ready for some serious work. Each pair of birds will start their nest's creation by bombing droplets of spit at the cave wall. The spit hardens over time, becoming like cement. These first horseshoe-shaped layers of spit act as a foundation. The pair then continues to craft the nest by adding long, thick strands of saliva, layer by layer, until a cup-shaped nest is formed. It takes about 35 days to finish the nest.

Eventually, the eggs hatch and the chicks take off, but the story doesn't end there. Their nests are edible, and some humans like to eat them! These saliva creations have been a prized food source in parts of Asia for thousands of years.

Once carefully harvested and cleaned, the nests can be eaten in dishes such as soup. They are an expensive delicacy, which some people believe can improve your health – although there is no scientific evidence of this. Unfortunately, collecting too many nests for food is causing the number of swiftlets to decrease in some places. Conservationists are now working to protect these amazing birds.

MUD NEST

A MUD PIE CASTLE

A fluffy, pale grey chick sits in the crater of an earthy mound. This baby American Flamingo is a new member of a large flock here in the Bahamas. The muddy nest where the chick sits was scraped together by its parents, who used their beaks to mould it, adding other natural materials such as straw, stones and feathers along the way. It's about 25 cm in height, with a dent at the top to cradle an egg. The flamingos live in a lagoon – a pool of shallow, salty water near the ocean. Atop the mound, the egg is protected against rising waters. The mud also keeps the egg at the right temperature, shielding it from the baking sun.

The breeding season depends on rainfall. Flamingos will only mate and make nests when there is a lot of rain to make sure there will be enough food for the birds and their young. Rain fills their habitat with food, such as algae and tiny sea creatures, like shrimp. It also creates the mud needed to build their nests.

The chick's downy feathers are dull compared to the adults' vibrant ones. As the chick grows, its feathers will gradually turn pink. This colour comes from the shrimp and other seafood it eats. The chick will be cared for not just by its parents, but also by other adults in the group, joining together with fellow babies in a creche.

INCUBATOR NEST

TOASTY EGGS

The Australian Brushturkey, with its startlingly red head and yellow wattle, is a scrappy bird. It lives across the east coast of Australia – from lush forests to scrubby open areas, whether high up in the mountains or down in the lowlands. It can even be found in back gardens. Wherever these birds make their home, they're always looking for the perfect spot for a nest.

Building the nest is a job for the male bird. He carefully chooses a spot on the ground and begins gathering material such as earth, dead plants and leaves. He uses his large feet and powerful legs to kick the materials into place to form a mound around 85 cm tall, and 3 to 4 m across. Female brushturkeys choose a mate based on how well they have built their mound.

If it's a really good mound, then more than one female will use it to lay her eggs. A single nest can hold up to 58 eggs in one season. Females will dig a hole in the mound to lay their eggs, which the male then covers up by piling even more natural materials on top. Eggs are laid about a month after the nest has been built, by which time the mound has become a mass of rotting compost.

But it's all part of the plan! The compost creates heat as it decomposes, which makes the perfect incubator for the eggs. To prevent it from becoming too hot, the male adds and removes layers of the mound to manage the temperature. After hatching, the chicks have to fight their way up through the mound to make it to the surface.

CLAY NEST

EGGS IN AN OVEN

In some scrubland in Argentina, in the boughs of a tree, sits a red dome. It looks like a piece of pottery, but it is actually the nest of a pair of Rufous Horneros – also known as red ovenbirds. The nest resembles a traditional clay oven, which is how these birds got their name.

Both mates helped to build the nest. Ferrying globs of wet mud bit by bit in their beaks, the birds began by laying a sturdy foundation on the tree branch. They constructed it in layers, and as well as mud, the first layers also contain straw, animal hair and cow poo. The birds continued to use mud to build up the curved walls, to form an 'oven' shape.

Once the dome was just about complete, the birds used their beaks to build an interior wall, creating a narrow corridor from the entrance. Safely tucked away behind the wall is a room for the eggs to be laid. The birds have lined the floor of this nest chamber with grasses and stems. The mud nest will keep the chicks cool under the baking sun and safe from rain.

During the breeding season, the pair will fiercely defend their nest from other birds. But once their chicks can fend for themselves, the nest is abandoned, and other birds can make use of it for their own chicks.

PILE IT ON

It's not uncommon for these birds to build new nests on top of old ones. They look like scoops of ice cream dolloped onto a cone.

PENDULUM NEST

MAKING AN ENTRANCE

In the dry savannah of Zimbabwe, a fluffy sack – the nest of a Cape Penduline Tit – droops down from a thorny shrub. For a month, two of these birds, which are only about 8 cm long, have used their beaks to weave the nest out of soft, downy plant fibres, wool from goats or sheep, and spider webs. They tease the material over and over again to create thick, felt-like walls. This material makes the nest strong and weather-resistant, but the sagging bag is still exposed to predators such as snakes. Luckily, the birds have a clever way to defend the nest.

The birds construct a main chamber in the nest where their eggs, and then chicks, will be cosy and secure. They then weave an obvious entrance into the side of the nest that any predators looking for an easy meal can stick their head into…but if they do, a dead end is all they'll find. This is a false entrance – a crafty trick to put hunters off the scent. The true entrance is just above the fake one, and to get into it, the birds pull it open with their beaks and feet. When inside, the entrance is closed safely behind them again.

SUPPORTIVE SIBLINGS

The birds usually lay between 4 to 8 eggs during the breeding season. Once the chicks hatch, the parents need help with the big job of feeding them. Their offspring from a previous breeding season will rejoin the nest to help provide food to the new baby birds.

BOWER POWER

A DECORATIVE DISPLAY

Nests aren't the only amazing structures that birds can build. In a wet Australian woodland, a male Satin Bowerbird has been busily making a structure called a bower. First, he created a round platform using sticks. Then, with more sticks and twigs, he thatched two curved walls, creating a short tunnel. The purpose of the bower is to attract a female.

To impress a female bowerbird, the male has gathered blue objects that are as alluring as his own rich, blue-black feathers. His collection of treasures includes blue parrot feathers, snail shells and iridescent insect bodies. A century ago, this bird would have only collected natural materials, but because of human pollution he has also gathered blue pieces of rubbish, such as plastic bottle tops, pieces of paper and shards of glass. Each object is carefully placed in a display around the bower. The bird also pastes the inside of the bower with a dark paint made of charcoal, berries and saliva.

The stage is now set. When an interested female approaches the decorated bower, the male bird leaps into a dance. He struts, bows and stretches his wings, all while making buzzing sounds and holding one of his found treasures in his beak. The female walks through the arched bower, and if she likes the sound of the song and the look of the display, she'll stay. Then, it's up to her to put together an actual nest for eggs, which she does by placing a shallow pile of sticks in a tree with a lining of leaves.

STOP, THIEF!

There's stiff competition over materials for displays. Younger males form gangs and will steal decorations from an older Satin Bowerbird's collection. They can even go as far as dismantling the bower!

NEST BUILDERS

HOW TO BUILD A CUP NEST

Cup nests are the most common shape of bird nest. They are found across the world. Although different birds make them in their own unique way, all cup nests are built to be strong and protect the bird's young effectively.

STEP 2

GATHER SUPPLIES

The bird collects nest-building materials such as grass, twigs or plant stems.

STEP 1

FIND A NEST SITE

A bird finds a sturdy place to build its nest, such as the forked boughs of a tree, or within a hedge. There should be enough cover to hide the nest from hunters.

STEP 3

BUILD A BASE

Using the gathered materials, the bird starts to construct the nest by creating a secure base platform.

STEP 4

WEAVE A CUP

From the base, the bird will then use materials like dried grass, twigs or moss to thatch the main cup of the nest, cleverly using its beak to twist everything into place. Some birds use mud to reinforce the cup.

STEP 5

LINE THE NEST

Next, it's time to line the inside of the cup. Depending on the bird, this inside layer could be made of soft materials such as feathers, hair or grass, or it could be lined with dried mud.

STEP 6

DECORATE THE NEST

Some birds add greenery such as grasses, leaves and moss around the outside of the nest for extra camouflage.

STEP 7

LAY EGGS

Now that the cup nest is built and ready, the female bird can lay her eggs.

GLOSSARY

algae – a plant-like organism without roots, leaves or stems, which grows in or around water.

aquatic – to do with water.

breeding season – a specific time when animals mate to ensure offspring are born at a time of year when there is plenty of food.

brood – a group of young birds who all hatched at the same time.

camouflage – to blend into the background, or to look like something else.

chamber – an enclosed space or room.

colony – a group of birds who all nest in the same location.

clutch – the number of eggs a bird lays in one nesting attempt. This can range from 1 to 18 eggs depending on the bird.

creche – a system where chicks are cared for together in a group, supervised by adult birds while their parents are away.

flight feathers – specific feathers that help a bird fly, they are often stiffer and larger than the other feathers on a bird's body.

floodplains – a flat area of land next to a river that regularly floods.

goslings – baby geese.

hatchling – a young animal that has recently hatched from an egg.

iridescent – shimmery rainbow colours that change when seen from different angles.

migrate – when an animal moves from one area to another, usually when the seasons change.

offspring – the children of a parent.

panoramic – a very wide view of a large area.

predator – an animal that hunts other animals to eat.

thatch – weaving together natural fibres such as straw or grass to create a denser material.

waterfowl – a bird that lives on or around a lake or river.

wattle – an extra bit of flesh that is not covered by feathers, which hangs under or around a bird's throat or head.

wetland – land that is normally covered in water for long periods of time.

INDEX

algae 12, 34, 46
American Flamingo 34–35
Australia Brushturkey 36–37
Bald Eagle 24–25
Barn Swallow 26–27
Blue-footed Booby 16–17
bower 42–43
breeding season 5, 11, 13, 23, 34, 39, 41, 46
burrow 18–19
Cactus Wren 8–9
camouflage 7, 15, 16, 31, 45, 46
Cape Penduline Tit 40–41
chicken 4
clay nest 38–39
clutch 4, 31, 46
colonies 11, 22, 28, 32, 46
Common Kingfisher 18–19
Common Tailorbird 14–15
cup nest 6–7, 44–45
domed nest 8–9
edible nest 32–33
flight feathers 21
floating nest 22–23
gosling 23, 46
Great Hornbill 20–21
Green Hermit hummingbird 30–31
hatchlings 5, 15, 25
hen 4
hermit nest 30–31
Horned Coot 12–13
incubator nest 36–37
Lappet-faced Vulture 29
Magpie Goose 22–23
migrate 8, 27, 46
mound nest 12–13
mud nest 26–27, 34–35, 38–39
pendulum nest 40–41,
platform nest 22–23
predator 4, 7, 8, 16, 19, 21, 29, 40, 46
Rufous Hornero (red ovenbird) 38–39
saliva 26, 32–33, 42
Satin Bowerbird 42–43
scrape nest 16–17
sealed nest 20–21
sociable nest 28–29
Sociable Weaver 28–29
Song Thrush 6–7
South African Pygmy Falcon 29
Southern Masked-Weaver 10–11
stitched nest 14–15
thatch 23, 29, 42, 45, 46
tunnel nest 18–19
waterfowl 25, 46
wattle 36, 46
wetland 22–23, 46
White-nest Swiftlet 32–33
woven nest 10–11

ABOUT THE AUTHOR

Lucy Menzies is an author and editor based in the UK. She has a decade of experience working in children's publishing.

ABOUT THE ILLUSTRATOR

Namasri Niumim is an illustrator living in Thailand with a degree in Fine Arts and Communication Design from the School of Architecture and Design at King Mongkut's University of Technology in Thonburi. She is the illustrator of *The Secret World of Spider Webs*.

ABOUT THE CONSULTANT

Douglas Russell is the Senior Curator responsible for the internationally renowned birds' egg and nest collections at the Natural History Museum in London. He is the author of several books on the subject of bird nests, including the *Smithsonian Handbook of Interesting Bird Nests and Eggs*.

First published in the United Kingdom in 2026 by
Thames & Hudson Ltd, 6–24 Britannia Street, London WC1X 9JD

Consultancy by Douglas Russell

EU Authorized Representative: Interart S.A.R.L.
19 rue Charles Auray, 93500 Pantin, Paris, France
productsafety@thameshudson.co.uk
interart.fr

A CIP catalogue record for this book is available from the British Library

ISBN 978-0-500-65394-4
01

Printed and bound in China by Toppan Leefung Printing Limited

MIX
Paper | Supporting responsible forestry
FSC® C104723

Be the first to know about our new releases,
exclusive content and author events by visiting
thamesandhudson.com
thamesandhudsonusa.com
thamesandhudson.com.au